DO NOT GO GENTLE

NEIL ASTLEY has been editing and publishing poetry for nearly 30 years. He founded Bloodaxe Books in 1978, and was given a D.Litt by Newcastle University for his pioneering work. He has published several other anthologies, including *Staying Alive: real poems for unreal times*, *Poetry with an Edge*, *New Blood* and *Pleased to See Me*, as well as two collections, *Darwin Survivor* (Poetry Book Society Recommendation) and *Biting My Tongue*. He won an Eric Gregory Award for his own poetry. His novel *The End of My Tether* was shortlisted for the Whitbread First Novel Award in 2002, and has just been published in paperback by Scribner.

DO NOT GO GENTLE

poems for funerals

edited by
NEIL ASTLEY

BLOODAXE BOOKS

ISBN: 1 85224 635 9

First published 2003 by
Bloodaxe Books Ltd,
Highgreen,
Tarset,
Northumberland NE48 1RP.

www.bloodaxebooks.com
For further information about Bloodaxe titles
please visit our website or write to
the above address for a catalogue.

Bloodaxe Books Ltd acknowledges
the financial assistance of
Arts Council England, North East.

Printed in Great Britain by
Bell & Bell Ltd., Glasgow

To everything there is a season, and a time to every purpose under heaven.

A time to be born and a time to die; a time to plant and a time to pluck up that which is planted;

A time to kill and a time to heal; a time to break down and a time to build up.

A time to weep and a time to laugh; a time to mourn and a time to dance.

A time to get and a time to lose; a time to keep and a time to cast away.

A time to rend and a time to sew; a time to keep silence, and a time to speak.

A time to love and a time to hate; a time of war, and a time of peace.

For that which befalleth the sons of men befalleth beasts; even one thing befalleth them: as the one dieth, so dieth the other; yea, they have all the breath; so that man hath no preeminence above a beast: for all is vanity.

KING JAMES BIBLE: ECCLESIASTES

What is born will die,
What has been gathered will be dispersed,
What has been accumulated will be exhausted,
What has been built up will collapse
And what has been high will be brought low.

TRADITIONAL BUDDHIST SCRIPTURE

CONTENTS

1 Stop All the Clocks
POEMS OF GRIEF

2 Lives Enriched
POEMS OF CELEBRATION

3 I Am Not There
BODY & SPIRIT

4 The Dying of the Light
PAIN & RESOLUTION

5 The Other Side
COMFORT & HAUNTING

6 Nothing Dies

1

Stop All the Clocks

POEMS OF GRIEF

Come sorrow, come! bring all thy cries,
All thy laments, and all thy weeping eyes!
Burn out, you living monuments of woe!
Sad sullen griefs, now rise and overflow!

JOHN FLETCHER

It is as natural to die as to be born; and to a little infant,
perhaps, the one is as painful as the other.

FRANCIS BACON

To die is only to be as we were before we were born;
yet no one feels any remorse, or regret, or repugnance,
in contemplating this last idea.

WILLIAM HAZLITT

Why do atheists have to say that one cannot rise from the dead?
Which is the more difficult, to be born or to be reborn?
That that which has never existed should exist, or that
that which has existed should exist again?
Is it more difficult to come into being than to return to it?

PASCAL

THE RIGHT POEM can help us share and bear the burden of immediate grief. The poems in this first section are deeply felt laments for loved ones. Each loss is particular to each writer, but the feelings evoked are universal, whether the person mourned is a parent or partner, child or close friend; and it may not matter who wrote a poem which speaks to you. George Herbert was a 17th-century country parson, but his poem 'Life' (17) has brought comfort to many agnostic parents who have lost children. When people find it difficult to talk, a poem's direct language can give voice to everyone's bewilderment. Reading it aloud, or hearing it read, may seem to open the wound but the intensity of that openly collective experience brings everyone closer as the poem's words speak for all.

Funeral Blues

Stop all the clocks, cut off the telephone,
Prevent the dog from barking with a juicy bone,
Silence the pianos and with muffled drum
Bring out the coffin, let the mourners come.

Let aeroplanes circle moaning overhead
Scribbling on the sky the message He Is Dead,
Put crêpe bows round the white necks of the public doves,
Let the traffic policemen wear black cotton gloves.

He was my North, my South, my East and West,
My working week and my Sunday rest,
My noon, my midnight, my talk, my song;
I thought that love would last for ever: I was wrong.

The stars are not wanted now: put out every one;
Pack up the moon and dismantle the sun;
Pour away the ocean and sweep up the wood.
For nothing now can ever come to any good.

W.H. AUDEN (1907-73)

Wept
(FROM *Elegy for an Artist*)

Never so *much* absence,
though, and not just absence,
never such a sense
of violated presence,
so much desolation,
so many desperate

last hopes refuted,
never such pure despair.
Surely I know by now
that each death demands
its own procedures
of mourning, but I can't

find those I need even
to begin mourning you:
so much affectionate
accord there was with you,
that to imagine
being without you

is impossibly
diminishing; I relied
on you to ratify
me, to reflect
and sanction with your life
who I might be in mine.

So restorative you were,
so much a response:
untenable that
the part of me you shared
with me shouldn't have you
actively a part of it.

Never so much absence,
so many longings ash,
as you are ash. Never
so cruel the cry within,
*Will I never again
be with you?* Ash. Ash.

C.K. WILLIAMS (*b.* 1936)
(for Bruce McGrew, 1937-99)

Memorial

Everywhere she dies. Everywhere I go she dies.
No sunrise, no city square, no lurking beautiful mountain
but has her death in it.
The silence of her dying sounds through
the carousel of language, it's a web
on which laughter stitches itself. How can my hand
clasp another's when between them
is that thick death, that intolerable distance?

She grieves for my grief. Dying, she tells me
that bird dives from the sun, that fish
leaps into it. No crocus is carved more gently
than the way her dying
shapes my mind. But I hear, too,
the other words,
black words that make the sound
of soundlessness, that name the nowhere
she is continuously going into.

Ever since she died
she can't stop dying. She makes me
her elegy. I am a walking masterpiece,
a true fiction
of the ugliness of death.
I am her sad music.

NORMAN MACCAIG (1910-96)

Comparisons

To all light things
I compared her; to
a snowflake, a feather.

I remember she rested
at the dance on my
arm, as a bird

on its nest lest
the eggs break, lest
she lean too heavily

on our love. Snow
melts, feathers
are blown away;

I have let
her ashes down
in me like an anchor.

R.S. THOMAS (1913-2000)

Remember

Remember me when I am gone away,
   Gone far away into the silent land;
   When you can no more hold me by the hand,
Nor I half turn to go yet turning stay.
Remember me when no more day by day
   You tell me of our future that you planned:
   Only remember me; you understand
It will be late to counsel then or pray.
Yet if you should forget me for a while
   And afterwards remember, do not grieve:
   For if the darkness and corruption leave
A vestige of the thoughts that once I had,
Better by far you should forget and smile
   Than that you should remember and be sad.

CHRISTINA ROSSETTI (1830-94)

The Five Stages of Grief

The night I lost you
someone pointed me towards
the Five Stages of Grief.
Go that way, they said,
it's easy, like learning to climb
stairs after the amputation.
And so I climbed.
Denial was first.
I sat down at breakfast
carefully setting the table
for two. I passed you the toast –
you sat there. I passed
you the paper – you hid
behind it.
Anger seemed more familiar.
I burned the toast, snatched
the paper and read the headlines myself.
But they mentioned your departure,
and so I moved on to
Bargaining. What could I exchange
for you? The silence
after storms? My typing fingers?
Before I could decide, *Depression*
came puffing up, a poor relation
its suitcase tied together
with string. In the suitcase
were bandages for the eyes
and bottles of sleep. I slid
all the way down the stairs
feeling nothing.
And all the time Hope
flashed on and off
in defective neon.
Hope was my uncle's middle name,
he died of it.
After a year I am still climbing,
though my feet slip
on your stone face.

The treeline
has long since disappeared;
green is a color
I have forgotten.
But now I see what I am climbing
towards; *Acceptance*
written in capital letters,
a special headline:
Acceptance,
its name is in lights.
I struggle on,
waving and shouting.
Below, my whole life spreads its surf,
all the landscapes I've ever known
or dreamed of. Below
a fish jumps: the pulse
in your neck.
Acceptance. I finally
reach it.
But something is wrong.
Grief is a circular staircase,
I have lost you.

LINDA PASTAN (*b.* 1932)

The Widower

For a season there must be pain –
For a little, little space
I shall lose the sight of her face,
Take back the old life again
While She is at rest in her place.

For a season this pain must endure,
For a little, little while
I shall sigh more often than smile
Till Time shall work me a cure,
And the pitiful days beguile.

15

For that season we must be apart,
For a little length of years,
Till my life's last hour nears,
And, above the beat of my heart,
I hear Her voice in my ears.

But I shall not understand –
Being set on some later love,
Shall not know her for whom I strove,
Till she reach me forth her hand,
Saying, 'Who but I have the right?'
And out of a troubled night
Shall draw me safe to the land.

RUDYARD KIPLING (1865-1936)

The Suicides

It is hard for us to enter
the kind of despair they must have known
and because it is hard we must get in by breaking
the lock if necessary for we have not the key,
though for them there was no lock and the surrounding walls
were supple, receiving as waves, and they drowned
though not lovingly; it is we only
who must enter in this way.

Temptations will beset us, once we are in.
We may want to catalogue what they have stolen.
We may feel suspicion; we may even criticise the decor
of their suicidal despair, may perhaps feel
it was incongruously comfortable.

Knowing the temptations then
let us go in
deep to their despair and their skin and know
they died because words they had spoken
returned always homeless to them.

JANET FRAME (*b.* 1924)

Life

I made a posie, while the day ran by:
Here will I smell my remnant out, and tie
        My life within this band.
But Time did beckon to the flowers, and they
By noon most cunningly did steal away,
        And wither'd in my hand.

My hand was next to them, and then my heart:
I took, without more thinking, in good part
        Times gentle admonition:
Who did so sweetly deaths sad taste convey,
Making my minde to smell my fatall day;
        Yet sugring the suspicion.

Farewell deare flowers, sweetly your time ye spent,
Fit, while ye liv'd, for smell or ornament,
        And after death for cures,
I follow straight without complaints or grief,
Since if my scent be good, I care not if
        It be as short as yours.

GEORGE HERBERT (1593-1633)

Epitaph Upon A Child That Died

Here she lies, a pretty bud,
Lately made of flesh and blood:
Who as soon fell fast asleep
As her little eyes did peep.
Give her strewings, but not stir
The earth that lightly covers her.

ROBERT HERRICK (1591-1674)

The Child Dying

Unfriendly friendly universe,
I pack your stars into my purse,
And bid you, bid you so farewell.
That I can leave you, quite go out,
Go out, go out beyond all doubt,
My father says, is the miracle.

You are so great, and I so small:
I am nothing, you are all:
Being nothing, I can take this way.
Oh I need neither rise nor fall,
For when I do not move at all
I shall be out of all your day.

It's said some memory will remain
In the other place, grass in the rain,
Light on the land, sun on the sea,
A flitting grace, a phantom face,
But the world is out. There is no place
Where it and its ghost can ever be.

Father, father, I dread this air
Blown from the far side of despair,
The cold cold corner. What house, what hold,
What hand is there? I look and see
Nothing-filled eternity,
And the great round world grows weak and old.

Hold my hand, oh hold it fast –
I am changing! – until at last
My hand in yours no more will change,
Though yours change on. You here, I there,
So hand in hand, twin-leafed despair –
I did not know death was so strange.

EDWIN MUIR (1887-1959)

On My First Sonne

Farewell, thou child of my right hand, and joy;
   My sinne was too much hope of thee, lov'd boy,
Seven yeeres tho'wert lent to me, and I thee pay,
   Exacted by thy fate, on the just day.
O, could I loose all father, now. For why
   Will man lament the state he should envie?
To have so soone scap'd worlds, and fleshes rage,
   And, if no other miserie, yet age?
Rest in soft peace, and, ask'd, say here doth lye
   BEN. JONSON his best piece of *poetrie*.
For whose sake, henceforth, all his vowes be such,
   As what he loves may never like too much.

BEN JONSON (1572/3-1637)

Light
(for Ciaran)

My little man, down what centuries
of light did you travel
to reach us here,
your stay so short-lived;

in the twinkling of an eye
you were moving on,
bearing our name and a splinter
of the human cross we suffer;

flashed upon us like a beacon,
we wait in darkness for that light
to come round, knowing at heart
you shine forever for us.

HUGH O'DONNELL (*b.*1951)

On the Death of a Child

The greatest griefs shall find themselves
           inside the smallest cage.
It's only then that we can hope to tame
           their rage,

The monsters we must live with. For it
           will not do
To hiss humanity because one human threw
Us out of heart and home. Or part

At odds with life because one baby failed
           to live.
Indeed, as little as its subject, is
           the wreath we give –

The big words fail to fit. Like giant boxes
Round small bodies. Taking up improper room,
Where so much withering is, and so much bloom.

D.J. ENRIGHT (1920-2003)

The Unquiet Grave

The wind doth blow today, my love,
    And a few small drops of rain;
I never had but one true-love;
    In cold grave she was lain.

'I'll do as much for my true-love
    As any young man may;
I'll sit and mourn all at her grave
    For a twelvemonth and a day.'

The twelvemonth and a day being up,
    The dead began to speak:
'O who sits weeping on my grave,
    And will not let me sleep?' –

"'Tis I, my love, sits on your grave,
    And will not let you sleep;
For I crave one kiss of your clay-cold lips,
    And that is all I seek.' –

'You crave one kiss of my clay-cold lips;
    But my breath smells earthy strong;
If you have one kiss of my clay-cold lips,
    Your time will not be long.

"'Tis down in yonder garden green,
    Love, where we used to walk,
The finest flower that ere was seen
    Is wither'd to a stalk.

'The stalk is wither'd dry, my love,
    So will our hearts decay;
So make yourself content, my love,
    Till God calls you away.'

ANONYMOUS

Remembrance

Cold in the earth – and the deep snow piled above thee!
    Far, far removed, cold in the dreary grave!
Have I forgot, my only love, to love thee,
    Severed at last by time's all-wearing wave?

Now, when alone, do my thoughts no longer hover
    Over the mountains, on that northern shore,
Resting their wings where heath and fern-leaves cover
    That noble heart for ever, ever more?

Cold in the earth, and fifteen wild Decembers
    From those brown hills have melted into spring –
Faithful indeed is the spirit that remembers
    After such years of change and suffering!

Sweet love of youth, forgive if I forget thee
    While the world's tide is bearing me along:
Sterner desires and darker hopes beset me,
    Hopes which obscure but cannot do thee wrong.

No other sun has lightened up my heaven,
  No other star has ever shone for me:
All my life's bliss from thy dear life was given –
  All my life's bliss is in the grave with thee.

But, when the days of golden dreams had perished,
  And even despair was powerless to destroy,
Then did I learn how existence could be cherished,
  Strengthened, and fed without the aid of joy.

Then did I check the tears of useless passion,
  Weaned my young soul from yearning after thine;
Sternly denied its burning wish to hasten
  Down to that tomb already more than mine!

And even yet, I dare not let it languish,
  Dare not indulge in memory's rapturous pain;
Once drinking deep of that divinest anguish,
  How could I seek the empty world again?

EMILY BRONTË (1818-48)

After the Burial

Yes, faith is a goodly anchor;
When skies are sweet as a psalm,
At the bows it lolls so stalwart,
In bluff, broad-shouldered calm.

And when over breakers to leeward
The tattered surges are hurled,
It may keep our head to the tempest,
With its grip on the base of the world.

But, after the shipwreck, tell me
What help in its iron thews,
Still true to the broken hawser,
Deep down among seaweed and ooze?

In the breaking gulfs of sorrow,
When the helpless feet stretch out
And find in the deeps of darkness
No footing so solid as doubt,

Then better one spar of Memory,
One broken plank of the Past,
That our human heart may cling to,
Though hopeless of shore at last!

To the spirit its splendid conjectures,
To the flesh its sweet despair,
Its tears o'er the thin-worn locket
With its anguish of deathless hair!

Immortal? I feel it and know it,
Who doubts it of such as she?
But that is the pang's very secret, –
Immortal away from me.

There's a narrow ridge in the graveyard
Would scarce stay a child in his race,
But to me and my thought it is wider
Than the star-sown vague of Space.

Your logic, my friend, is perfect,
Your morals most drearily true;
But, since the earth clashed on *her* coffin,
I keep hearing that, and not you.

Console if you will, I can bear it;
'Tis a well-meant alms of breath;
But not all the preaching since Adam
Has made Death other than Death.

It is pagan; but wait till you feel it, –
That jar of our earth, that dull shock
When the ploughshare of deeper passion
Tears down to our primitive rock.

Communion in spirit! Forgive me,
But I, who am earthy and weak,
Would give all my incomes from dreamland
For a touch of her hand on my cheek.

That little shoe in the corner,
So worn and wrinkled and brown,
With its emptiness confutes you
And argues your wisdom down.

JAMES RUSSELL LOWELL (1819-91)

Especially When It Snows

especially when it snows
and every tree
has its dark arms and widespread hands
full of that shining angelfood

especially when it snows
and every footprint
makes a dark lake
among the frozen grass

especially when it snows darling
and tough little robins
beg for crumbs
at golden-spangled windows

ever since we said goodbye to you
in that memorial garden
where nothing grew
except the beautiful blank-eyed snow

and little Caitlin crouched to wave goodbye to you
down in the shadows

especially when it snows
and keeps on snowing

especially when it snows
and down the purple pathways of the sky
the planet staggers like King Lear
with his dead darling in his arms

especially when it snows
and keeps on snowing

ADRIAN MITCHELL (*b.* 1932)
(for Boty Goodwin, 1966-95)

2

Lives Enriched

POEMS OF CELEBRATION

O how shall I warble myself for the dead one there I loved?
And how shall I deck my song for the large sweet soul that has gone?
And what shall my perfume be for the grave of him I love?

Sea-winds blown from east and west,
Blown from the Eastern sea and blown from the Western sea,
till there on the prairies meeting,
These and with these and the breath of my chant,
I'll perfume the grave of him I love.

WHITMAN

And death shall have no dominion...
Though lovers be lost love shall not.

DYLAN THOMAS

That which is of the sea is going to the sea:
it is going to the place from whence it came –
From the mountain the swift-rushing torrent,
and from our body the soul whose motion
is inspired by love.

RUMI

CELEBRATION is the uplifting counterweight to grief. Our lives were enriched – and are still enriched – by the person we're mourning. One of their gifts was humour, and in two of the poems here by American writers, the poets project their comic selves into fantasy funerals, Langston Hughes even scripting bluesy words to be 'hollered' by his female mourners in 'As Befits a Man' (33), while William Carlos Williams attacks convention and cant in 'Tract' (34), calling for the kind of honest simplicity typical of his own life and work. Critic Jahan Ramazani says we need these kinds of disturbingly modern poems 'because our society often sugarcoats mourning in dubious comfort, or retreats from it in embarrassed silence'. To be true to life, we may need the poet to throw a cat amongst the mourning doves. And we should be ourselves, urges Joyce Grenfell, 'So sing as well' (33).

Because He Lived

Because he lived, next door a child
To see him coming often smiled,
And thought him her devoted friend
Who gladly gave her coins to spend.

Because he lived, a neighbor knew
A clump of tall delphiniums blue
And oriental poppies red
He'd given for a flower bed.

Because he lived, a man in need
Was grateful for a kindly deed
And ever after tried to be
As thoughtful and as fine as he.

Because he lived, ne'er great or proud
Or known to all the motley crowd,
A few there were whose tents were pitched
Near his who found their lives enriched.

EDGAR A. GUEST (1881-1959)

Epitaph on a Friend

An honest man here lies at rest,
The friend of man, the friend of truth,
The friend of age, and guide of youth:
Few hearts like his, with virtue warm'd,
Few heads with knowledge so inform'd;
If there's another world, he lives in bliss;
If there is none, he made the best of this.

ROBERT BURNS (1759-96)

The Good

The good are vulnerable
As any bird in flight,
They do not think of safety,
Are blind to possible extinction
And when most vulnerable
Are most themselves.
The good are real as the sun,
Are best perceived through clouds
Of casual corruption
That cannot kill the luminous sufficiency
That shines on city, sea and wilderness,
Fastidiously revealing
One man to another,
Who yet will not accept
Responsibilities of light.
The good incline to praise,
To have the knack of seeing that
The best is not destroyed
Although forever threatened.
The good go naked in all weathers,
And by their nakedness rebuke
The small protective sanities
That hide men from themselves.
The good are difficult to see
Though open, rare, destructible;
Always, they retain a kind of youth,
The vulnerable grace
Of any bird in flight,
Content to be itself,
Accomplished master and potential victim,
Accepting what the earth or sky intends.
I think that I know one or two
Among my friends.

BRENDAN KENNELLY (*b.* 1936)

When a Friend

When a friend dies, part
of oneself splits off
and spins into the outer dark.
No use calling it back.
No use saying I miss you.
Part of one's body has been riven.
One recollects gestures,
mostly trivial. The way
he pinched a cigarette,
the way he crouched on a chair.
Now he is less than a living flea.
Where has he gone, this person
whom I loved? He is vapor now;
he is nothing. I remember
talking to him about the world.
What a rich place it became
within our vocabulary. I did not
love it half so much until
he spoke of it, until it was sifted
through the adjectives of our discussion.
And now my friend is dead.
His warm hand has been reversed.
His movements across a room
have been erased. How I wish
he was someplace specific. He
is nowhere. He is absence.
When he spoke of the things
he loved – books, music, pictures,
the articulation of idea –
his body shook as if a wire
within him suddenly surged.
In passion, he filled the room.
Where has he gone, this friend
whom I loved? The way he shaved,
the way he cut his hair, even
the way he squinted when he talked,
when he embraced idea, held it –
all vanished. He has been reduced
to memory. The books he loved,

I see them on my shelves. The words
he spoke still group around me. But
this is chaff. This is the container
now that heart has been scraped out.
He is defunct now. His body is less
than cinders; less than a sentence
after being whispered. He is the zero
from which a man has vanished. He
was the smartest, most vibrant,
like a match suddenly struck, flaring;
now he is sweepings in a roadway.
Where is he gone? He is nowhere.
My friends, I knew a wonderful man,
these words approximate him,
as chips of stone approximate
a tower, as wind approximates a song.

STEPHEN DOBYNS (*b.* 1941)
(for Ellis Settle, 1924-93)

Cleopatra's Lament for Antony

          Noblest of men, woo't die?
Hast thou no care of me, shall I abide
In this dull world, which in thy absence is
No better than a sty? O, see, my women:
The crown o' the earth doth melt.   [*Antony dies.*]
                      My lord?
O, wither'd is the garland of the war,
The soldier's pole is fall'n: young boys and girls
Are level now with men: the odds is gone,
And there is nothing left remarkable
Beneath the visiting moon.

[...]

29

No more but e'en a woman, and commanded
By such poor passion as the maid that milks,
And does the meanest chares. It were for me
To throw my sceptre at the injurious gods,
To tell them that this world did equal theirs,
Till they had stol'n our jewel. All's but naught:
Patience is sottish, and impatience does
Become a dog that's mad: then is it sin,
To rush into the secret house of death,
Ere death dare come to us? How do you, women?
What, what, good cheer! Why, how now, Charmian?
My noble girls! Ah, women, women. Look,
Our lamp is spent, it's out. Good sirs, take heart,
We'll bury him: and then, what's brave, what's noble,
Let's do it after the high Roman fashion,
And make death proud to take us. Come, away,
This case of that huge spirit now is cold.
Ah, women, women! come, we have no friend
But resolution, and the briefest end.

WILLIAM SHAKESPEARE (1564-1616)
(*Antony and Cleopatra*, IV.xv. 59-68, 73-91)

Dirge for Fidele

Fear no more the heat o' th' sun,
   Nor the furious winter's rages'
Thou thy worldly task has done,
   Home art gone and ta'en thy wages.
Golden lads and girls all must,
As chimney-sweepers, come to dust.

Fear no more the frown o' th' great,
   Thou art past the tyrant's stroke
Care no more to clothe and eat,
   To thee the reed is as the oak.
The sceptre, learning, physic, must
All follow this, and come to dust.

Fear no more the lightning-flash,
    Nor th' all-dreaded thunder-stone;
Fear not slander, censure rash.
    Thou has finish'd joy and moan.
All lovers young, all lovers must
Consign to thee and come to dust.

No exorciser harm thee!
Nor no witchcraft charm thee!
Ghost unlaid forbear thee!
Nothing ill come near thee!
Quiet consummation have,
And renowned be thy grave!

WILLIAM SHAKESPEARE (1564-1616)
(*Cymbeline*, IV.ii.258-81)

'We say the dead depart'

We say the dead depart but can't say where
And can't imagine being nowhere, time
Full-stopped. But absence
Is here and now, we rub along
Shoulder to shoulder with the vacancies
The dead have left, doing the best we can
Less well with poorer means and greater need
In a worsened world, to fill them. This week
Everyone sees the deficit, time running out
Everyone has the dead man's kindness in their view
Everyone needing it, no one
Meeting a friend of his this week
Has had an unkind word. And how alive
The world continues to be with things the dead man loved
Last week, goldfinches, say,
A charm, and how bereft they look, not so well admired, they want
Their due and look to us
The bereaved, his understudies.

DAVID CONSTANTINE (*b.* 1944)

Not, how did he die, but how did he live?
Not, what did he gain, but what did he give?
These are the units to measure the worth
Of a man as a man, regardless of birth.
Not what was his church, nor what was his creed?
But had he befriended those really in need?
Was he ever ready, with word of good cheer,
To bring back a smile, to banish a tear?
Not what did the sketch in the newspaper say,
But how many were sorry when he passed away?

ANONYMOUS

from In Memoriam A.H.H.
(four stanzas from LXXXV)

This truth came borne with bier and pall,
   I felt it, when I sorrowed most.
    'Tis better to have loved and lost
Than never to have loved at all – [...]

But I remained, whose hopes were dim,
   Whose life, whose thoughts were little worth,
    To wander on a darkened earth,
Where all things round me breathed of him. [...]

Whatever ways my days decline,
   I felt and feel, though left alone,
    His being working in mine own,
The footsteps of his life in mine; [...]

And so my passion hath not swerved
   To works of weakness, but I find
    An image comforting the mind,
And in my grief a strength reserved.

ALFRED, LORD TENNYSON (1809-92)

As Befits a Man

I don't mind dying –
But I'd hate to die all alone!
I want a dozen pretty women
To holler, cry, and moan.

I don't mind dying
But I want my funeral to be fine:
A row of long tall mamas
Fainting, fanning, and crying.

I want a fish-tail hearse
And sixteen fish-tail cars,
A big brass band
And a whole truck load of flowers.

When they let me down,
Down into the clay,
I want the women to holler:
Please don't take him away!
Ow-ooo-oo-o!
Don't take daddy away!

LANGSTON HUGHES (1902-67)

from Joyce: By Herself and Her Friends

If I should go before the rest of you
Break not a flower nor inscribe a stone,
Nor when I'm gone speak in a Sunday voice
But be the usual selves that I have known.
        Weep if you must,
        Parting is hell,
But life goes on,
So sing as well.

JOYCE GRENFELL (1910-79)

Tract

I will teach you my townspeople
how to perform a funeral –
for you have it over a troop
of artists –
unless one should scour the world –
you have the ground sense necessary.

See! the hearse leads.
I begin with a design for a hearse.
For Christ's sake not black –
nor white either – and not polished!
Let it be weathered – like a farm wagon –
with gilt wheels (this could be
applied fresh at small expense)
or no wheels at all:
a rough dray to drag over the ground.

Knock the glass out!
My God – glass, my townspeople!
For what purpose? Is it for the dead
to look out or for us to see
how well he is housed or to see
the flowers or the lack of them –
or what?
To keep the rain and snow from him?
He will have a heavier rain soon:
pebbles and dirt and what not.
Let there be no glass –
and no upholstery, phew!
and no little brass rollers
and small easy wheels on the bottom –
my townspeople what are you thinking of?

A rough plain hearse then
with gilt wheels and no top at all.
On this the coffin lies
by its own weight.

                    No wreaths please –
especially no hot house flowers.
Some common memento is better,
something he prized and is known by:
his old clothes – a few books perhaps –
God knows what! You realise
how we are about these things
my townspeople –
something will be found – anything
even flowers if he had come to that.
So much for the hearse.

For heaven's sake though see to the driver!
Take off the silk hat! In fact
that's no place at all for him –
up there unceremoniously
dragging our friend out to his own dignity!
Bring him down – bring him down!
Low and inconspicious! I'd not have him ride
on the wagon at all – damn him –
the undertaker's understrapper!
Let him hold the reins
and walk at the side
and inconspicuously too!

Then briefly as to yourselves:
Walk behind – as they do in France,
seventh class, or if you ride
Hell take curtains! Go with some show
of inconvenience; sit openly –
to the weather as to grief.
Or do you think you can shut grief in?
What – from us? We who have perhaps
nothing to lose? Share with us
share with us – it will be money
in your pockets.
                    Go now
I think you are ready.

WILLIAM CARLOS WILLIAMS (1883-1963)

Gravy

No other word will do. For that's what it was. Gravy.
Gravy, these past ten years.
Alive, sober, working, loving and
being loved by a good woman. Eleven years
ago he was told he had six months to live
at the rate he was going. And he was going
nowhere but down. So he changed his ways
somehow. He quit drinking! And the rest?
After that it was *all* gravy, every minute
of it, up to and including when he was told about,
well, some things that were breaking down and
building up inside his head. 'Don't weep for me,'
he said to his friends. 'I'm a lucky man.
I've had ten years longer than I or anyone
expected. Pure gravy. And don't forget it.'

RAYMOND CARVER (1939-88)

Haiku

Skylark
sings all day,
and day not long enough.

BASHŌ (1644-94)
translated from the Japanese
by Lucien Stryk & Takashi Ikemoto

3

I Am Not There

BODY & SPIRIT

When a man is born, it is but the embodiment of a spirit.
When the spirit is embodied, there is life, and when the spirit
disperses, there is death.

LAO-TSE

If you are a Buddhist and believe in rebirth, then death is just a
change of physical body, rather like the way one swaps old clothes
for new ones once they are worn out. When our physical support is
no longer capable of keeping us alive due to internal and external
causes, the time has come to give it up and take a new one. In these
conditions, dying does not mean that we cease to exist.

14TH DALAI LAMA

Death is in reality spiritual birth, the release of the spirit from
from the prison of the senses into the freedom of God, just as
physical birth is the release of the baby from the prison of the
womb into the freedom of the world. While childbirth causes pain
and suffering to the mother, for the baby it brings liberation.

RUMI

THE BODY DIES but the spirit survives is the message of many poems of
mourning: *'Do not stand at my grave and weep;/ I am not there. I do not
sleep.'* These include poems by writers of different faiths, from the Zen
Buddhist composers of Japanese haiku to the ascetic classical Arab poet,
Abu al-Ala al-Ma'arri.

Henry van Dyke's short meditation on time (39), written for engraving
on a sun-dial, was read at the funeral of Diana, Princess of Wales, by her
sister Jane, while her other sister Sarah chose to read Mary Lee Hall's
'Turn Again to Life' (39). Written at least 50 years ago, the anonymous
'Do not stand at my grave and weep' (38) has been attributed, at various
times, to J.T. Wiggins, Mary E. Fry and Marianne Reinhardt, and more
recently to a British soldier killed in Northern Ireland who left a copy for
his relatives. The short poems in this book by Rumi are extracted from
much longer works. Jalâluddin Rumi was a master of the Sufi tradition,
the mystical branch of Islam; his teachings inspired the Whirling Dervishes.

37

'Do not stand at my grave and weep'

Do not stand at my grave and weep;
I am not there. I do not sleep.
I am a thousand winds that blow.
I am the diamond glints on snow.
I am the sunlight on ripened grain.
I am the gentle autumn rain.

When you awaken in the morning's hush
I am the swift uplifting rush
Of quiet birds in circled flight.
I am the soft stars that shine at night.
Do not stand at my grave and cry;
I am not there. I did not die.

ANONYMOUS

Song

When I am dead, my dearest,
Sing no sad songs for me;
Plant thou no roses at my head,
Nor shady cypress tree:
Be the green grass above me
With showers and dewdrops wet;
And if thou wilt, remember,
And if thou wilt, forget.

I shall not see the shadow,
I shall not feel the rain;
I shall not hear the nightingale
Sing on, as if in pain;
And dreaming through the twilight
That doth not rise nor set,
Haply I may remember,
And haply may forget.

CHRISTINA ROSSETTI (1830-94)

Turn Again to Life

If I should die and leave you here a while,
Be not like others, sore undone, who keep
Long vigils by the silent dust, and weep.
For my sake – turn again to life and smile,
Nerving thy heart and trembling hand to do
Something to comfort other hearts than thine.
Complete those unfinished tasks of mine
And I, perchance, may therein comfort you.

MARY LEE HALL

For Katrina's Sun Dial

Time is too slow for those who wait,
Too swift for those who fear,
Too long for those who grieve,
Too short for those who rejoice,
But for those who love, time is
Eternity.

HENRY VAN DYKE (1852-1933)

'Thinking I enjoyed the pleasures of life'

Thinking I enjoyed the pleasures of life
I myself was enjoyed by life.

Thinking I didn't need to burn off my sins,
I myself was burnt up.

Thinking that I passed the time,
I myself was passing on.

Greed didn't grow old & leave my body,
I myself grew old.

BHARTRHARI (7th century)
translated from the Sanskrit by John Cort

Demiurge

They say that reality exists only in the spirit
that corporal existence is a kind of death
that pure being is bodiless
that the idea of the form precedes the form substantial.

But what nonsense it is!
as if any Mind could have imagined a lobster
dozing in the under-deeps, then reaching out a savage and iron claw!

Even the mind of God can only imagine
those things that have become themselves:
bodies and presences, here and now, creatures with a foothold in
        creation
even if it is only a lobster on tiptoe.

Religion knows better than philosophy.
Religion knows that Jesus was never Jesus
till he was born from a womb, and ate soup and bread
and grew up, and became, in the wonder of creation, Jesus,
with a body and with needs, and a lovely spirit.

D.H. LAWRENCE (1885-1930)

In the End Is the Body

In the end is the body – what we know
as inspiration departs before
the final assault of pain and decay.
Even the carpenter's son from Nazareth
could not, in the end, overcome
the body's claims though he knew
inspiration more than most.

And don't imagine his mother
was indifferent to the hammer smashing
the arrangement of bone and sinew she
had held in hers at his beginning.
She wished him back unpierced, smelling
of sawdust and sweat. He was the one
she'd hoped would close her eyes in the end.

In the end my mother lay
body-bound, curled like a foetus,
fretting for a peppermint, a sip of whiskey,
the pillow turned this way and that,
and she a woman who, buoyant in silk
and shingled hair, stood on the hill
at Fiesole reciting her Browning to the wind.

GAIL HOLST-WARHAFT (b. 1941)

41

Sonnet LXXXIX

(FROM *100 Love Sonnets*)

When I die, I want your hands on my eyes:
I want the light and wheat of your beloved hands
to pass their freshness over me once more:
I want to feel the softness that changed my destiny.

I want you to live while I wait for you, asleep.
I want your ears still to hear the wind, I want you
to sniff the sea's aroma that we loved together,
to continue to walk on the sand we walk on.

I want what I love to continue to live,
and you whom I love and sang above everything else
to continue to nourish, full-flowered:

so that you can reach everything my love directs you to,
so that my shadow can travel along in your hair,
so that everything can learn the reason for my song.

PABLO NERUDA (1904-73)
translated from the Spanish by Stephen Tapscott

Haiku

When I go,
guard my tomb well,
grasshopper.

ISSA (1763-1827)
translated from the Japanese
by Lucien Stryk & Takashi Ikemoto

The Soul Driven from the Body

The soul driven from the body
Mourns the memory it leaves behind.

A dove hit in flight sadly turns
Its neck and sees its nest destroyed.

ABU AL-ALA AL-MA'ARRI (973-1057/8)
translated from the Arabic by
Abdullah al-Udhari & George Wightman

'I'm the one who has the body'

I'm the one who has the body,
you're the one who holds the breath.

You know the secret of my body,
I know the secret of your breath.

That's why your body
is in mine.

You know
and I know, Rāmanātha,

the miracle

of your breath
in my body.

DEVARA DASIMAYYA (10th century Indian)
translated from the Kannada by A.K. Ramanujan

The Paradox

Our death implicit in our birth,
We cease, or cannot be;
And know when we are laid in earth
We perish utterly.

And equally the spirit knows
The indomitable sense
Of immortality, which goes
Against all evidence.

See faith alone, whose hand unlocks
All mystery at a touch,
Embrace the awful Paradox
Nor wonder overmuch.

RUTH PITTER (1897-1992)

'Everything you see'

Everything you see has its roots in the unseen world.
    The forms may change, yet the essence remains the same.
Every wonderful sight will vanish, every sweet word will fade,
    But do not be disheartened,
The source they come from is eternal, growing,
    Branching out, giving new life and new joy.
Why do you weep?
    The source is within you
And this whole world is springing up from it.

RUMI (1207-73)
translated from the Persian by Andrew Harvey

4

The Dying of the Light

PAIN & RESOLUTION

The world today hangs on a single thread, and that thread
is the psyche of man.

JUNG

Since nature's works be good, and death doth serve
As nature's work, why should we fear to die?
Since fear is vain, but when it may preserve,
Why should we fear that which we cannot fly?

PHILIP SIDNEY

For many of us, religious rituals are no longer adequate to the
complexities of mourning for the dead...In the power and intricacy
of the modern elegy, we can discover some of the twentieth
century's most sophisticated thinking about grief, some of its most
impassioned articulations of it...We need elegies that, while imbued
with grief, can hold up to the acid suspicions of our moment.

JAHAN RAMAZANI

MANY MODERN POETS write as agnostics or unbelievers, and in trying to
make sense of death they are confronting not only loss but fear of extinc-
tion. This section has several contemporary poems which doubters and
sceptics may find helpful, especially those amongst us who aren't sure what
we believe, whose grief over loss is the more intense for not knowing what
happens to the soul after death. Such poems offer not solace or comfort but
honest engagement with fears we all share. In his extended elegy 'Le Petit
Salvié' (53-56), American poet C.K. Williams wrestles with the meaning of
death, helping us make sense of no sense, mirroring our own anxieties and
contradictions (too long to read in full, the two extracts here offer scope
for further selection). Seamus Heaney called Philip Larkin's 'Aubade' (52)
'the definitive post-Christian English poem, one that abolishes the soul's
traditional pretension to immortality'. Other poets would assert that absence
of life after death is as questionable as its presence. But however various
and contradictory these poems, their message chimes with Larkin's famous
words (in 'An Arundel Tomb'), proving 'Our almost-instinct almost true:/
What will survive of us is love.'

Do Not Go Gentle into That Good Night

Do not go gentle into that good night,
Old age should burn and rave at close of day;
Rage, rage against the dying of the light.

Though wise men at their end know dark is right,
Because their words had forked no lightning they
Do not go gentle into that good night.

Good men, the last wave by, crying how bright
Their frail deeds might have danced in a green bay,
Rage, rage against the dying of the light.

Wild men who caught and sang the sun in flight,
And learn, too late, they grieved it on its way,
Do not go gentle into that good night.

Grave men, near death, who see with blinding sight
Blind eyes could blaze like meteors and be gay,
Rage, rage against the dying of the light.

And you, my father, there on the sad height,
Curse, bless, me now with your fierce tears, I pray.
Do not go gentle into that good night.
Rage, rage against the dying of the light.

DYLAN THOMAS (1914-53)

Invictus

Out of the night that covers me,
    Black as the Pit from pole to pole,
I thank whatever gods may be
    For my unconquerable soul.

In the fell clutch of circumstance
    I have not winced nor cried aloud.
Under the bludgeonings of chance
    My head is bloody, but unbowed.

Beyond this place of wrath and tears
    Looms but the horror of the shade,
And yet the menace of the years
    Finds, and shall find, me unafraid.

It matters not how strait the gate,
    How charged with punishments the scroll,
I am the master of my fate:
    I am the captain of my soul.

W.E. HENLEY (1849-1903)

Et in Arcadia

Living is here
And now. I
Look forward, see
Today tomorrow
A yesterday
Of what was I
When we were.

All is recalling: how
Our vision of what's gone
Changes with each new Now
As we change with what's done
And our perspectives change.
Life, they say, must go on
To alter all, to alter
In recollection
That shadow of her shadow,
All of her that I am.

The sun on a polluted river,
May morning by a flowing Thames,
A lace of trees, their leaves beginning,
And we two strangers holding hands
Beside a theatre yet a-building,
By broken bricks and iron bones
Of weathered bomb-sites weeding over
In sunlight that's presaging summer,
A summer that has come, and gone.

Et in Arcadia
Ego. As evening
Leads her shadow on
And, diamond, a star
Increases with the wane
Of light to promise a
Different beginning,
I am to thank whatever for
The fortune of day.

I am changing: she does not.
How can I change and she not change?
Those words, Till death do us part,
Too late I understand.
I see things in a different dark,
All things that nothing can explain.

DAVID WRIGHT (1920-94)

On Parting with My Wife, Janina

Women mourners were giving their sister to fire.
And fire, the same as we looked at together,
She and I, in marriage through long years,
Bound by an oath for good or ill, fire
In fireplaces in winter, campfires, fires of burning cities,
Elemental, pure, from the beginnings of the Earth,
Was taking away her streaming hair, gray,
Seized her lips and her neck, engulfed her, fire
That in human languages designates love.
I thought nothing of languages. Or of words of prayer.

I loved her, without knowing who she really was.
I inflicted pain on her, chasing my illusion.
I betrayed her with women, though faithful to her only.
We lived through much happiness and unhappiness,
Separations, miraculous rescues. And now, this ash.
And the sea battering the shore when I walk the empty boulevard.
And the sea battering the shore. And ordinary sorrow.

How to resist nothingness? What power
Preserves what once was, if memory does not last?
For I remember little. I remember so very little.
Indeed, moments restored would mean the Last Judgment
That is adjourned from day to day, by Mercy perhaps.

Fire, liberation from gravity. An apple does not fall,
A mountain moves from its place. Beyond the fire-curtain,
A lamb stands in the meadow of indestructible forms.
The souls in Purgatory burn. Heraclitus, crazy,
Sees the flame consuming the foundations of the world.
Do I believe in the Resurrection of the Flesh? Not of this ash.

I call, I beseech: elements, dissolve yourselves!
Rise into the other, let it come, kingdom!
Beyond the earthly fire compose yourselves anew!

CZESLAW MILOSZ (*b*. 1911)
translated from the Polish by Czeslaw Milosz & Robert Hass

from **When You Died**

1

When you died
I went through the rain
carrying my nightmare
to register the death.

A well-groomed healthy gentleman
safe within his office
said – Are you the widow?

Couldn't he have said
Were you his wife?

2

After the first shock
I found I was
solidly set in my flesh.
I was an upright central pillar,
the soft flesh melted round me.
My eyes melted
spilling the inexhaustible essence of sorrow.
The soft flesh of the body
melted onto chairs and into beds
dragging its emptiness and pain.

I lodged inside holding myself upright,
warding off the dreadful deliquescence.

3

November.
Stooping under muslins
of grey rain I fingered
through ribbons of wet grass,
traced stiff stems down to the wormy earth
and one by one snapped off

the pale surviving flowers; they would ride
with him, lie on the polished plank
above his breast.

People said – Why do you not
follow the coffin?
Why do you not
have any funeral words spoken?
Why not
send flowers from a shop?

[...]

5

When you died
I did not for the moment
think about myself;
I grieved deeply and purely for your loss,
that you had lost your life.
I grieved bitterly for your mind destroyed,
your courage thrown away,
your senses aborted under the amazing skin
no one would ever touch again.

I grieve still
that we'd have grown
even more deeply close and old together
and now shall not.

PAMELA GILLILAN (1918-2001)

Aubade

I work all day, and get half-drunk at night.
Waking at four to soundless dark, I stare.
In time the curtain-edges will grow light.
Till then I see what's really always there:
Unresting death, a whole day nearer now,
Making all thought impossible but how
And where and when I shall myself die.
Arid interrogation: yet the dread
Of dying, and being dead,
Flashes afresh to hold and horrify.

The mind blanks at the glare. Not in remorse
– The good not done, the love not given, time
Torn off unused – nor wretchedly because
An only life can take so long to climb
Clear of its wrong beginnings, and may never;
But at the total emptiness for ever,
The sure extinction that we travel to
And shall be lost in always. Not to be here,
Not to be anywhere,
And soon; nothing more terrible, nothing more true.

This is a special way of being afraid
No trick dispels. Religion used to try,
That vast moth-eaten musical brocade
Created to pretend we never die,
And specious stuff that says *No rational being*
Can fear a thing it will not feel, not seeing
That this is what we fear – no sight, no sound,
No touch or taste or smell, nothing to think with,
Nothing to love or link with,
The anaesthetic from which none come round.

And so it stays just on the edge of vision,
A small unfocused blur, a standing chill
That slows each impulse down to indecision.
Most things may never happen: this one will,
And realisation of it rages out
In furnace-fear when we are caught without

People or drink. Courage is no good:
It means not scaring others. Being brave
Lets no one off the grave.
Death is no different whined at than withstood.

Slowly light strengthens, and the room takes shape.
It stands plain as a wardrobe, what we know,
Have always known, know that we can't escape,
Yet can't accept. One side will have to go.
Meanwhile telephones crouch, getting ready to ring
In locked-up offices, and all the uncaring
Intricate rented world begins to rouse.
The sky is white as clay, with no sun.
Work has to be done.
Postmen like doctors go from house to house.

PHILIP LARKIN (1922-85)

from Le Petit Salvié

We didn't know how ill you were...we knew how ill but hid it...
    we didn't know how ill you were...
Those first days when your fever rose...if we'd only made you go
    into the hospital in Brive...
Perhaps you could have had another year...but the way you'd let
    death touch your life so little,
the way you'd learned to hold your own mortality before you like
    an unfamiliar, complex flower...
Your stoicism had become so much a part of your identity, your
    virtue, the system of your self-regard;
if we'd insisted now, you might have given in to us, when we didn't,
    weren't we cooperating
with what wasn't just your wish but your true passion never to be
    dying, sooner dead than dying?
You did it, too: composed a way from life directly into death, the
    ignoble scribblings between elided.

It must be some body-thing, some species-thing, the way it comes
to take me from so far,
this grief that tears me so at moments when I least suspect it's there,
wringing tears from me
I'm not prepared for, had no idea were even there in me, this most
unmanly gush I almost welcome,
these cries so general yet with such power of their own I'm stunned
to hear them come from me.
Walking through the street, I cry, talking later to a friend, I try not
to but I cry again,
working at my desk I'm taken yet again, although, again, I don't
want to be, not now, not again,
though that doesn't mean I'm ready yet to let you go...what it does
mean I don't think I know,
nor why I'm so ill prepared for this insistence, this diligence with
which consciousness afflicts us.

I imagine you rising to something like heaven: my friend who died
last year is there to welcome you.
He would know the place by now, he would guide you past the
ledges and the thorns and terror.
Like a child I am, thinking of you rising in the rosy clouds and
being up there with him,
being with your guru Baba, too, the three of you, all strong men,
all partly wild children,
wandering through my comforting child's heaven, doing what you're
supposed to do up there forever.
I tell myself it's silly, all of this, absurd, what we sacrifice in attain-
ing rational mind,
but there you are again, glowing, grinning down at me from some-
where in the heart of being,
ablaze with wonder and a child's relief that this after all is how
astonishingly it finishes.

In my adult mind, I'm reeling, lost – I can't grasp anymore what I
even think of death.
I don't know even what we hope for: ecstasy? bliss? or just release
from being, not to suffer anymore.
At the grave, the boring rabbi said that you were going to eternal
rest: rest? why rest?
Better say we'll be absorbed into the 'Thou', better be consumed
in light, in Pascal's 'Fire'!
Or be taken to the Godhead, to be given meaning now, at last, the
meaning we knew eluded us.

God, though, Godhead, Thou, even fire: all that is gone now, gone
the dark night arguments,
gone the partial answers, the very formulations fail; I grapple for
the questions as *they* fail.
Are we to be redeemed? When? How? After so much disbelief, will
something be beyond us to receive us?

Redemption is in life, 'beyond' unnecessary: it is radically demeaning
to any possible divinity
to demand that life be solved by yet another life: we're compressed
into this single span of opportunity
for which our gratitude should categorically be presumed; this is
what eternity for us consists of,
praise projected from the soul, as love first floods outward to the
other then back into the self...
Yes, yes, I try to bring you to this, too; yes, what is over now is
over; yes, we offer thanks,
for what you had, for what we all have: this portion of eternity is
no different from eternity,
they both contract, expand, cast up illusion and delusion and all
the comfort that we have is love,
praise, the grace not to ask for other than we have...yes and yes,
but this without conviction, too.
[...]

How ambiguous the triumphs of our time, the releasing of the
intellect from myth and magic.
We've gained much, we think, from having torn away corrupted
modes of aggrandizement and giantism,
those infected and infecting errors that so long held sway and so
bloated our complacencies
that we would willingly inflict even on our own flesh the crippling
implications of our metaphysic.
How much we've had to pay, though, and how dearly had to suffer
for our liberating dialectics.
The only field still left to us to situate our anguish and uncertainty
is in the single heart,
and how it swells, the heart, to bear the cries with which we troubled
the startled heavens.
Now we have the air, transparent, and the lucid psyche, and gazing
inward, always inward, to the wound.

The best evidence I have of you isn't my memory of you, or your
    work, although I treasure both,
and not my love for you which has too much of me in it as subject,
    but the love others bore you,
bear you, especially Vikki, who lived out those last hard years with
    you, the despairs and fears,
the ambivalences and withdrawals, until that final week of fever that
    soaked both your pillows.
Such a moving irony that your last days finally should have seared
    the doubt from both of you.
Sometimes it's hard to tell exactly whom I cry for – you, that last
    night as we left you there,
the way you touched her with such solicitude, or her, the desolation
    she keeps coming to:
'*I've been facing death, touched death, and now I have a ghost I love
    and who loves me.*'

Genevieve, your precious Gen, doesn't quite know when to cry, or
    how much she's supposed to cry,
or how to understand those moments when it passes, when she's
    distracted into play and laughter
by the other kids or by the adults who themselves don't seem to
    grasp this terrible non-game.
At the cemetery, I'm asked to speak to her, comfort her: never more
    impossible to move beyond cliché.
We both know we're helplessly embedded in ritual: you wanted her,
    I tell her, to be happy,
that's all, all her life, which she knows, of course, but nods to, as
    she knows what I don't say,
the simplest self-revealing truths, your most awful fear, the brutal
    fact of your mortality:
how horribly it hurt to go from her, how rending not being here
    to help bear this very pain.
[…]

C.K. WILLIAMS (*b.* 1936)
(*for Paul Zweig, 1935-84*)

The Minister

We're going to need the minister
to help this heavy body into the ground.

But he won't dig the hole;
others who are stronger and weaker will have to do that.
And he won't wipe his nose and his eyes;
others who are weaker and stronger will have to do that.
And he won't bake cakes or take care of the kids –
women's work. Anyway,
what would they do at a time like this
if they didn't do that?

No, we'll get the minister to come
and take care of the words.

He doesn't have to make them up,
he doesn't have to say them well,
he doesn't have to like them
so long as they agree to obey him.

We have to have the minister
so the words will know where to go.

Imagine them circling and circling
the confusing cemetery.
Imagine them roving the earth
without anywhere to rest.

ANNE STEVENSON (*b.* 1933)

A Last Marriage

The children gone, grown into other arms,
Man of her heart and bed gone underground,
Powder and chunks of ash in a shamefast urn,
Her mother long since buried in a blue gown,
Friends vanishing downward from the highway crash,
Slow hospital dooms, or a bullet in the head,
She came at last alone into her overgrown
Shapeless and forlorn garden. Death was there
Too, but tangible. She hacked and dragged away
Horrors of deadwood, webbed and sagging foliage,
Self-strangling roots, vines, suckers, arboreal
Deformities in viperish coils. Sweat, anger, pity
Poured from her. And her flesh was jabbed by thorns,
Hair jerked by twigs, eyes stung by mould and tears.

But day by day in the afterbath she recovered stillness.
Day by day the disreputable garden regained
Its green tenderness. They wooed one another. The living
Responses issued from clean beds of earth.
It was a new marriage, reclusive, active, wordless.
Early each morning even in rain she walked
The reviving ground where one day she would knock and enter.
She took its green tribute into her arms and rooms.
Through autumn the pruned wood gave her ceremonial
Fires, where she saw lost faces radiant with love.
Beyond the window, birds passed and the leaves with them.
Now was a season to sit still with time to know,
Drawing each breath like a fine crystal of snow.

VIRGINIA HAMILTON ADAIR (*b.* 1913)

5

The Other Side

COMFORT & HAUNTING

He is made one with Nature: there is heard
His voice in all her music, from the moan
Of thunder, to the song of night's sweet bird;
He is a presence to be felt and known
In darkness and in light, from herb and stone.

SHELLEY

I feel her presence in the common day,
In that slow dark that widens every eye.
She moves as water moves, and comes to me,
Stayed by what was, and pulled by what would be.

THEODORE ROETHKE

The dead are often just as living to us as the living are,
only we cannot get them to believe it. They can come to us,
but till we die we cannot go to them. To be dead is to be unable
to understand that one is alive.

SAMUEL BUTLER

This existence of ours is as transient as autumn clouds.
To watch the birth and death of beings is like looking
at the movements of a dance.
A lifetime is like a flash of lightning in the sky
Rushing by, like a torrent down a steep mountain.

BUDDHA

WHEN WE FEEL the presence of someone who has died, whether through
dreams or imagination, second sight or sixth sense, such hauntings can
offer comfort. In several of the poems here, the writers come to terms
with loss by acting out a remembered or imaginary encounter; or they
learn to think of the person they mourn not as dead but as how they were
when most alive.

Notes from the Other Side

I divested myself of despair
and fear when I came here.

Now there is no more catching
one's own eye in the mirror,

there are no bad books, no plastic,
no insurance premiums, and of course

no illness. Contrition
does not exist, nor gnashing

of teeth. No one howls as the first
clod of earth hits the casket.

The poor we no longer have with us.
Our calm hearts strike only the hour,

and God, as promised, proves
to be mercy clothed in light.

JANE KENYON (1947-95)

The Reassurance

About ten days or so
After we saw you dead
You came back in a dream.
I'm all right now you said.

And it was you, although
You were fleshed out again:
You hugged us all round then,
And gave your welcoming beam.

How like you to be kind,
Seeking to reassure.
And, yes, how like my mind
To make itself secure.

THOM GUNN (*b.* 1929)

Breath

People keep telling me you're still here
I can talk to you. Sometimes I believe them.
If breath could mist the mirror you'd appear.

Till I remember the oxygen hissing
from your abandoned mask, making me lightheaded
as I sat, stroked your hand, witnessing

the still blow of morphia winning that last bout,
the long pause, the final angry sigh
as if the world had breathed me out.

PATRICIA POGSON (*b.* 1944)

Oh

Oh my, Harold Brodkey, of all people, after all this time, appearing
     to me,
so long after his death, so even longer since our friendship, our
     last friendship,
the third or fourth, the one anyway when the ties between us
     definitively frayed,
(Oh, Harold's a handful, another of his ex-friends sympathized, to
     my relief);

Harold Brodkey, at a Christmas eve dinner, of all times and places,
because of my nephew's broken nose, of all reasons, which he suffered
     in an assault,
the bone shattered, reassembled, but healing a bit out of plumb,
and when I saw him something Harold wrote came to mind, about
     Marlon Brando,

how until Brando's nose was broken he'd been pretty, but after he
     was beautiful,
and that's the case here, a sensitive boy now a complicatedly handsome
     young man
with a sinewy edge he hadn't had, which I surely remark because
     of Harold,
and if I spoke to the dead, which I don't, or not often, I might
     thank him:

It's pleasant to think of you, Harold, of our good letters and talks;
I'm sorry we didn't make it up that last time, I wanted to but I was
     worn out
by your snits and rages, your mania to be unlike and greater than
     anyone else,
your preemptive attacks for inadequate acknowledgement of your
     genius...

But no, leave it alone, Harold's gone, truly gone, and isn't it un-
     forgivable, vile,
to stop loving someone, or to stop being loved; we don't mean to
     lose friends,
but someone drifts off, and we let them, or they renounce us, or
     we them, or we're hurt,
like flowers, for god's sake, when really we're prideful brutes, as
     blunt as icebergs.

Until something like this, some Harold Brodkey wandering into
        your mind,
as exasperating as ever, and, oh my, as brilliant, as charming, unwound
        from his web
to confront you with how ridden you are with unthought regret,
        how diminished,
how well you'll know you'll clink on to the next rationalization, the
        next loss, the next lie.

C.K. WILLIAMS (*b.* 1936)

Years go by
(FROM *Poem without a title*)

Father I say. Dad? You again?
I take your arm, your elbow,
I turn you around in the dark and I say

go back now, you're sleepwalking again,
you're talking out loud again, talking in tongues
and your dream is disturbing my dream.

And none of this is any of your apples,
and even now as the centuries begin to happen
I can say: go away, you and all your violence.

Shush, now, old man.
Time to go back to your seat in the one-and-nines,
to your black bench on the Esplanade,

your name and your dates on a metal plate, back
to your own deckchair on the pier, your very own
kitchen chair tipped back on the red kitchen tiles

and you asleep, your feet up on the brass fender
and the fire banked, your cheek cocked
to the radio set, this is the 9 o'clock news Dad.

It's time. It's long past it.
Time to go back up the long pale corridor
there's no coming back from.

KEN SMITH (1938-2003)

I See You Dancing, Father

No sooner downstairs after the night's rest
And in the door
Than you started to dance a step
In the middle of the kitchen floor.

And as you danced
You whistled.
You made your own music
Always in tune with yourself.

Well, nearly always, anyway.
You're buried now
In Lislaughtin Abbey
And whenever I think of you

I go back beyond the old man
Mind and body broken
To find the unbroken man.
It is the moment before the dance begins,

Your lips are enjoying themselves
Whistling an air.
Whatever happens or cannot happen
In the time I have to spare
I see you dancing, father.

BRENDAN KENNELLY (*b.* 1936)

In Memory of My Mother

I do not think of you lying in the wet clay
Of a Monaghan graveyard; I see
You walking down a lane among the poplars
On your way to the station, or happily

Going to second Mass on a summer Sunday –
You meet me and you say:
'Don't forget to see about the cattle – '
Among your earthiest words the angels stray.

And I think of you walking along a headland
Of green oats in June,
So full of repose, so rich with life –
And I see us meeting at the end of a town

On a fair day by accident, after
The bargains are all made and we can walk
Together through the shops and stalls and markets
Free in the oriental streets of thought.

O you are not lying in the wet clay,
For it is a harvest evening now and we
Are piling up the ricks against the moonlight
And you smile up at us – eternally.

PATRICK KAVANAGH (1904-67)

The Dead

The dead are always looking down on us, they say,
while we are putting on our shoes or making a sandwich,
they are looking down through the glass-bottom boats of heaven
as they row themselves slowly through eternity.

They watch the tops of our heads moving below on earth,
and when we lie down in a field or on a couch,
drugged perhaps by the hum of a warm afternoon,
they think we are looking back at them,

which makes them lift their oars and fall silent
and wait, like parents, for us to close our eyes.

BILLY COLLINS (*b.* 1941)

Resurrection

Is it true that after this life of ours we shall one day be awakened
by a terrifying clamour of trumpets?
Forgive me, God, but I console myself
that the beginning and resurrection of all of us dead
will simply be announced by the crowing of the cock.

After that we'll remain lying down a while...
The first to get up
will be Mother... We'll hear her
quietly laying the fire,
quietly putting the kettle on the stove
and cosily taking the teapot out of the cupboard.
We'll be home once more.

VLADIMÍR HOLAN (1905-80)
translated from the Czech by George Theiner

Eden Rock

They are waiting for me somewhere beyond Eden Rock:
My father, twenty-five, in the same suit
Of Genuine Irish Tweed, his terrier Jack
Still two years old and trembling at his feet.

My mother, twenty-three, in a sprigged dress
Drawn at the waist, ribbon in her straw hat,
Has spread the stiff white cloth over the grass.
Her hair, the colour of wheat, takes on the light.

She pours tea from a Thermos, the milk straight
From an old H.P. sauce bottle, a screw
Of paper for a cork; slowly sets out
The same three plates, the tin cups painted blue.

The sky whitens as if lit by three suns.
My mother shades her eyes and looks my way
Over the drifted stream. My father spins
A stone along the water. Leisurely,

They beckon to me from the other bank.
I hear them call, 'See where the stream-path is!
Crossing is not as hard as you might think.'

I had not thought that it would be like this.

CHARLES CAUSLEY (*b.* 1917)

Inside Our Dreams

Where do people go to when they die?
Somewhere down below or in the sky?
'I can't be sure,' said Grandad, 'but it seems
They simply set up home inside our dreams.'

JEANNE WILLIS (*b.* 1959)

Song

Hari is a dhobi
                takes in
all stained souls.

                In the river
of his love,
                with the soap
of his peace
                glowing
iridescent in the sun

                he washes
every one.
                No envious smear
returns.
                The souls
he's done

                are like muslin
when worn, says Meera.

MEERA (16th century poet-saint)
*translated from the Rajasthani version of Hindu
by Shama Futehally*

Haiku

White butterfly
darting among pinks –
whose spirit?

SHIKI (1867-1902)
*translated from the Japanese
by Lucien Stryk & Takashi Ikemoto*

6

Nothing Dies

RELEASE & LETTING GO

Your essence was not born and will not die. It is neither
being nor nonbeing. It is not a void nor does it have form.
It experiences neither pleasure nor pain. If you ponder what
it is in you that feels the pain of this sickness, and beyond that
you do not think or desire or ask anything, and if your mind
dissolves like vapour in the sky, then the path to rebirth is
blocked and the moment of instance release has come.

BASSUI

Total annihilation is impossible. We are the prisoners of an
infinity without outlet, wherein nothing perishes, wherein
everything is dispersed, but nothing lost. Neither a body nor
a thought can drop out of the universe, out of time and space.
Not an atom of our flesh, not a quiver of our nerves, will go
where they will cease to be, for there is no place where anything
ceases to be...It is as contradictory to the nature of our reason
and probably of all imaginable reason to conceive
nothingness as to conceive limits to infinity.

MAURICE MAETERLINCK

MANY POEMS show our lives as following the natural cycles of the Earth,
and when autumn comes, it is time to let go, for winter will be followed
by rebirth in spring. We must believe in the possibility of resurrection at
the same time as we accept the inevitability of withdrawal, for death is not
only inescapable but a defining force in life itself; as American poet Louise
Glück has written: 'Human beings must be taught to love / silence and
darkness.' The poems in this section reflect a range of beliefs: for some,
resurrection is followed by reincarnation: 'Why cling to one life till it is
oiled and ragged?' asks Rumi (82); while for others it involves living on
through children or spiritual renewal. That sense of *letting go* also informs
poems which view death as a welcome release from painful illness or from
the prison of old age, but death can also be welcomed when life has been
lived to the full: 'I don't want to end up simply having visited this world,'
writes Mary Oliver in 'When Death Comes' (83).

After Great Pain

After great pain a formal feeling comes –
The nerves sit ceremonious like tombs;
The stiff Heart questions – was it He that bore?
And yesterday – or centuries before?

The feet mechanical
Go round a wooden way
Of ground or air or Ought, regardless grown,
A quartz contentment like a stone.

This is the hour of lead
Remembered if outlived,
As freezing persons recollect the snow –
First chill, then stupor, then the letting go.

EMILY DICKINSON (1830-96)

In Blackwater Woods

Look, the trees
are turning
their own bodies
into pillars

of light,
are giving off the rich
fragrance of cinnamon
and fulfillment,

the long tapers
of cattails
are bursting and floating away over
the blue shoulders

of the ponds,
and every pond,
no matter what its
name is, is

nameless now.
Every year
everything
I have ever learned

in my lifetime
leads back to this: the fires
and the black river of loss
whose other side

is salvation,
whose meaning
none of us will ever know.
To live in this world

you must be able
to do three things:
to love what is mortal;
to hold it

against your bones knowing
your own life depends on it;
and, when the time comes to let it go,
to let it go.

MARY OLIVER (*b.* 1935)

from Song of Myself

A child said *What is the grass?* fetching it to me with full hands;
How could I answer the child? I do not know what it is any more
    than he.

I guess it must be the flag of my disposition, out of hopeful green
    stuff woven.

Or I guess it is the handkerchief of the Lord,
A scented gift and remembrancer designedly dropt,
Bearing the owner's name someway in the comers, that we may
     see and remark, and say *Whose?*

Or I guess the grass is itself a child, the produced babe of the
     vegetation.

Or I guess it is a uniform hieroglyphic,
And it means, Sprouting alike in broad zones and narrow zones,
Growing among black folks as among white,
Kanuck, Tuckahoe, Congressman, Cuff, I give them the same, I
     receive them the same.

And now it seems to me the beautiful uncut hair of graves.

Tenderly will I use you curling grass,
It may be you transpire from the breasts of young men,
It may be if I had known them I would have loved them,
It may be you are from old people, or from offspring taken soon
     out of their mothers' laps,
And here you are the mothers' laps.

This grass is very dark to be from the white heads of old mothers,
Darker than the colorless beards of old men,
Dark to come from under the faint red roofs of mouths.

O I perceive after all so many uttering tongues,
And I perceive they do not come from the roofs of mouths for nothing.
I wish I could translate the hints about the dead young men and
     women,
And the hints about old men and mothers, and the offspring taken
     soon out of their laps.

What do you think has become of the young and old men?
And what do you think has become of the women and children?

They are alive and well somewhere,
The smallest sprout shows there is really no death,
And if ever there was it led forward life, and does not wait at the
     end to arrest it,
And ceas'd the moment life appear'd.

All goes onward and outward, nothing collapses,
And to die is different from what any one supposed, and luckier.

WALT WHITMAN (1819-82)

72

Unmarked Boxes

Don't grieve. Anything you lose comes round
in another form. The child weaned from mother's milk
now drinks wine and honey mixed.

God's joy moves from unmarked box to unmarked box,
from cell to cell. As rainwater, down into flowerbed.
As roses, up from ground.
Now it looks like a plate of rice and fish,
now a cliff covered with vines,
now a horse being saddled.
It hides within these,
till one day it cracks them open.

Part of the self leaves the body when we sleep
and changes shape. You might say, 'Last night
I was a cypress tree, a small bed of tulips,
a field of grapevines.' Then the phantasm goes away.
You're back in the room.
I don't want to make anyone fearful.
Hear what's behind what I say.

Tatatumtum, tatum, tatadum.
There's the light gold of wheat in the sun
and the gold of bread made from that wheat.
I have neither. I'm only talking about them,

as a town in the desert looks up
at stars on a clear night.

RUMI (1207-73)
translated from the Persian by Coleman Barks with John Moyne

The Creation

Now that I know you are gone
I have to try, like Rauschenberg,
to rub out, line by line,
your picture, feeling as I rub
the maker's most inhuman
joy, seeing as I rub
the paper's slow, awful return
to possibility.
Five times you screamed and won
from your short body a big boy
or a tall girl to join
the rest of us here,
and now let daughter or son
wear all that's left of your face
when this drawing's undone.

It is hard, heavy work.
The pencil indented the grain
of the paper, and I scour
a long time on a cheekbone
that doesn't want to disappear,
hoping my fingers won't learn
its line from going over and over
it. I replace your chin
with dead white.
Once, in a little vain
coquettishness, you joined
your party late, hair down
to your waist, and let the men
watch you twist it around
to a blonde rope and pin
the richness of its coils
into a familiar bun.
And now I make you bald
with my abrasion.
The hours we had to drink
before you'd put the dinner on!
My eraser's wet with sweat
as it moves on a frown

of long, tipsy decision:
were we all so drunk
it didn't matter, or should you strain
the Mornay sauce?
Already we are worn,
the eraser and I, and we
are nearing your eyes. Your garden
was what you saw each morning,
and your neighbors, making fun
other oversolicitude:
'I swear that woman
digs her plants up every day
to see if their roots have grown.'
You tucked the ticklish roots
of half-grown youngsters, back in
and pressed the tilth around them.
Your eyes were an intervention.
You saw your words begin
a moody march to the page
when you tried to write what you'd seen
in poems you brought out one by one
to show us, getting braver
slowly – yes, too slowly. When
you finally sent some off –
too slowly – a magazine
took one and printed it
too slowly; you had just gone.
If I raise my head from this work
what I see is that the sun
is shining anyway,
and will continue to shine
no matter whose pale Dutch blue
eyes are closed or open,
no matter what graphite memories
do or do not remain,
so I erase and don't
look up again.
When I answer the phone
I don't any longer expect
your jerky conversation –
one funny little comment,
then silence until I began

trying to fill it myself;
at last the intention
would appear, 'Come for dinner
and help me entertain
someone I'm scared of.' It was hard
to believe you were often
really sick and afraid.
You heard the tune
of our feelings, I think,
over the phone, even.
You liked a joke.
You loved Beethoven.
And this is the end of your ear.
I see your nose redden
with summer allergies,
wrinkle at your husband's pun
and then straighten and fade.
What is left of you is graven,
almost, into one kind of smile.
I don't think I can mourn
much more than I already have
for this loved irritant – prune
pucker, with ends of lips
pulled up. More than your grin
it lasts, and with it lasts
a whole characterization
I can't dispose of
unless I rub clear through and ruin
this piece of anti-art.
When our repartee would run
too fast, or someone's anecdote
run long, or someone mention
a book you hadn't read,
that smile meant you were hidden.
It meant you needed time
to think of something clever or mean,
or that you thought we'd gone too far
from the gentle and sane.
It meant you were our wise,
dear, vulnerable, human
friend, as true and false as life
would let you be, and when

I move you that much farther from
your self to generalization
there is a blur
and your smile stops. This thing is done.

Swept empty by a cyclone
inside, I lift the paper.
But before I blow it clean,
sketched now in rubber crumbs,
another face is on it – mine,
Sneak, Poet, Mon-
ster,
trying to rob you with words.

Your death was your own.

MONA VAN DUYN (*b.* 1921)

Heredity

I am the family face;
Flesh perishes, I live on,
Projecting trait and trace
Through time to times anon,
And leaping from place to place
Over oblivion.

The years-heired feature that can
In curve and voice and eye
Despise the human span
Of durance – that is I;
The eternal thing in man,
That heeds no call to die.

THOMAS HARDY (1840-1928)

'Good Night, Willie Lee,
I'll See You in the Morning'

Looking down into my father's
dead face
for the last time
my mother said without
tears, without smiles
without regrets
but with civility
'Good night, Willie Lee, I'll see you
in the morning.'
And it was then I knew that the healing
of all our wounds
is forgiveness
that permits a promise
of our return
at the end.

ALICE WALKER (*b.* 1944)

Kaddish

Mother of my birth, for how long were we together
in your love and my adoration of your self?
For the shadow of a moment, as I breathed your pain
and you breathed my suffering. As we knew
of shadows in lit rooms that would swallow the light.

Your face beneath the oxygen tent was alive
but your eyes closed, your breathing hoarse.
Your sleep was with death. I was alone
with you as when I was young
but now only alone, not with you,
to become alone forever, as I was learning
watching you become alone.

Earth now is your mother, as you were mine, my earth,
my sustenance and my strength,
and now without you I turn to your mother
and seek from her that I may meet you again
in rock and stone. Whisper to the stone,
I love you. Whisper to the rock, I found you.
Whisper to the earth, Mother, I have found her,
and I am safe and always have been.

DAVID IGNATOW (1914-97)

A Marriage

We met
        under a shower
of bird-notes.
        Fifty years passed,
love's moment
        in a world in
servitude to time.
        She was young;
I kissed with my eyes
        closed and opened
them on her wrinkles.
        'Come' said death,
choosing her as his
        partner for
the last dance. And she,
        who in life
had done everything
        with a bird's grace,
opened her bill now
        for the shedding
of one sigh no
        heavier than a feather.

R.S. THOMAS (1913-2000)

Three Elegiac Poems

I

Let him escape hospital and doctor,
    the manners and odors of strange places,
    the dispassionate skills of experts.

Let him go free of tubes and needles,
    public corridors, the surgical white
    of life dwindled to poor pain.

Foreseeing the possibility of life without
    possibility of joy, let him give it up.

Let him die in one of the old rooms
    of his living, no stranger near him.

Let him go in peace out of the bodies
    of his life –
    flesh and marriage and household.

From the wide vision of his own windows
    let him go out of sight; and the final

time and light of his life's place be
    last seen before his eyes' slow
    opening in the earth.

Let him go like one familiar with the way
    into the wooded and tracked and
    furrowed hill, his body.

II

I stand at the cistern in front of the old barn
in the darkness, in the dead of winter,
the night strangely warm, the wind blowing,
rattling an unlatched door.
I draw the cold water up out of the ground, and drink.

At the house the light is still waiting.
An old man I have loved all my life is dying
in his bed there. He is going
slowly down from himself.
In final obedience to his life, he follows
his body out of our knowing.
Only his hands, quiet on the sheet, keep
a painful resemblance to what they no longer are.

III

He goes free of the earth.
The sun of his last day sets
clear in the sweetness of his liberty.

The earth recovers from his dying,
the hallow of his life remaining
in all his death leaves.

Radiances know him. Grown lighter
than breath, he is set free
in our remembering. Grown brighter

than vision, he goes dark
into the life of the hill
that holds his peace.

He is hidden among all that is,
and cannot be lost.

WENDELL BERRY (*b.* 1934)
(for Harry Erdman Perry, 1881-1965)

In the Nursing Home

She is like a horse grazing
a hill pasture that someone makes
smaller by coming every night
to pull the fences in and in.

She has stopped running wide loops,
stopped even the tight circles.
She drops her head to feed; grass
is dust, and the creekbed's dry.

Master, come with your light
halter. Come and bring her in.

JANE KENYON (1947-95)

'Why cling'

Why cling to one life
till it is soiled and ragged?

The sun dies and dies
squandering a hundred lives
every instant

God has decreed life for you
and He will give
    another and another and another.

RUMI (1207-73)
translated from the Persian by Daniel Liebert

When Death Comes

When death comes
like the hungry bear in autumn;
when death comes and takes all the bright coins from his purse

to buy me, and snaps the purse shut;
when death comes
like the measle-pox;

when death comes
like an iceberg between the shoulder blades,

I want to step through the door full of curiosity, wondering:
what is it going to be like, that cottage of darkness?

And therefore I look upon everything
as a brotherhood and a sisterhood,
and I look upon time as no more than an idea,
and I consider eternity as another possibility,

and I think of each life as a flower, as common
as a field daisy, and as singular,

and each name a comfortable music in the mouth,
tending, as all music does, toward silence,

and each body a lion of courage, and something
precious to the earth.

When it's over, I want to say: all my life
I was a bride married to amazement.
I was the bridegroom, taking the world into my arms.

When it's over, I don't want to wonder
if I have made of my life something particular and real.
I don't want to find myself sighing and frightened,
or full of argument.

I don't want to end up simply having visited this world.

MARY OLIVER (b. 1935)

83

Come, Death

Why dost thou dally, Death, and tarry on the way?
When I have summoned thee with prayers and tears, why dost
       thou stay?
Come, Death, and carry now my soul away.

Wilt thou not come for calling, must I show
Force to constrain thy quick attention to my woe?
I have a hand upon thy Coat, and will
Not let thee go.

How foolish are the words of the old monks,
In Life remember Death.
Who would forget
Thou closer hangst on every finished breath?
How vain the work of Christianity
To teach humanity
Courage in its mortality.
Who would not rather die
And quiet lie
Beneath the sod
With or without a god?

Foolish illusion, what has Life to give?
Why should man more fear Death than fear to live?

STEVIE SMITH (1902-71)

'Death be not proud'

Death be not proud, though some have called thee
Mighty and dreadfull, for, thou art not soe,
For, those, whom thou think'st, thou dost overthrow,
Die not, poore death, nor yet canst thou kill mee;
From rest and sleepe, which but thy pictures bee,
Much pleasure, then from thee, much more must flow,
And soonest our best men with thee doe goe,
Rest of their bones, and soules deliverie.

Thou art slave to Fate, chance, kings, and desperate men,
And dost with poyson, warre, and sicknesse dwell,
And poppie, or charmes can make us sleepe as well,
And better than thy stroake; why swell'st thou then?
One short sleepe past, wee wake eternally,
And death shall be no more, Death thou shalt die.

JOHN DONNE (1572-1631)

Nothing Is Lost

Nothing is lost.
We are too sad to know that, or too blind;
Only in visited moments do we understand:
It is not that the dead return –
They are about us always, though unguessed.

This pencilled Latin verse
You dying wrote me, ten years past and more,
Brings you as much alive to me as the self you wrote it for,
Dear father, as I read your words
With no word but Alas.

Lines in a letter, lines in a face
Are faithful currents of life: the boy has written
His parents across his forehead, and as we burn
Our bodies up each seven years,
His own past self has left no plainer trace.

Nothing dies.
The cells pass on their secrets, we betray them
Unknowingly: in a freckle, in the way
We walk, recall some ancestor,
And Adam in the colour of our eyes.

Yes, on the face of the new born,
Before the soul has taken full possession,
There pass, as over a screen, in succession
The images of other beings:
Face after face looks out, and then is gone.

Nothing is lost, for all in love survive.
I lay my cheek against his sleeping limbs
To feel if he is warm, and touch in him
   Those children whom no shawl could warm,
      No arms, no grief, no longing could revive.

   Thus what we see, or know,
Is only a tiny portion, at the best,
Of the life in which we share; an iceberg's crest
   Our sunlit present, our partial sense,
      With deep supporting multitudes below.

ANNE RIDLER (1912-2001)

Let Evening Come

Let the light of late afternoon
shine through chinks in the barn, moving
up the bales as the sun moves down.

Let the cricket take up chafing
as a woman takes up her needles
and her yarn. Let evening come.

Let dew collect on the hoe abandoned
in long grass. Let the stars appear
and the moon disclose her silver horn.

Let the fox go back to its sandy den.
Let the wind die down. Let the shed
go black inside. Let evening come.

To the bottle in the ditch, to the scoop
in the oats, to air in the lung
let evening come.

Let it come, as it will, and don't
be afraid. God does not leave us
comfortless, so let evening come.

JANE KENYON (1947-95)

from Autumn Journal

Sleep, my body, sleep, my ghost,
  Sleep, my parents and grandparents,
And all those I have loved most:
  One man's coffin is another's cradle.
Sleep, my past and all my sins,
  In distant snow or dried roses
Under the moon for night's cocoon will open
  When day begins.
Sleep, my fathers, in your graves
  On upland bogland under heather;
What the wind scatters the wind saves,
  A sapling springs in a new country.
Time is a country, the present moment
  A spotlight roving round the scene;
We need not chase the spotlight,
  The future is the bride of what has been.
Sleep, my fancies and my wishes,
  Sleep a little and wake strong,
The same but different and take my blessing –
  A cradle-song.

LOUIS MACNEICE (1907-63)

A Celtic Blessing

Deep peace of the running wave to you,
Deep peace of the flowing air to you,
Deep peace of the quiet earth to you,
Deep peace of the shining stars to you,
Deep peace of the Son of Peace to you.
May the road rise to meet you;
May the wind be always at your back;
May the sun shine warm upon your face;
May the rains fall softly upon your fields.
    Until we meet again,
May God hold you in the hollow of His hand.

[ANONYMOUS]

No Need

I see an empty place at the table.
Whose? Who else's? Who am I kidding?
The boats waiting. No need for oars
or a wind. I've left the key
in the same place. You know where.
Remember me and all we did together.
Now, hold me tight. That's it. Kiss me
hard on the lips. There. Now
let me go, my dearest. Let me go.
We shall not meet again in this life,
so kiss me goodbye now. Here, kiss me again.
Once more. There. That's enough.
Now, my dearest, let me go.
It's time to be on the way.

RAYMOND CARVER (1939-88)

This Is What I Wanted to Sign Off With

You know what I'm
like when I'm sick: I'd sooner
curse than cry. And people don't often
know what they're saying in the end.
Or I could die in my sleep.

So I'll say it now. Here it is.
Don't pay any attention
if I don't get it right
when it's for real. Blame that
on terror and pain
or the stuff they're shooting
into my veins. This is what I wanted to
sign off with. Bend
closer, listen, I love you.

ALDEN NOWLAN (1933-83)

Late Fragment

And did you get what
you wanted from this life, even so?
I did.
And what did you want?
To call myself beloved, to feel myself
beloved on the earth.

RAYMOND CARVER (1939-88)

Dead Woman

If suddenly you do not exist,
if suddenly you no longer live,
I shall live on.

I do not dare,
I do not dare to write it,
if you die.

I shall live on.

For where a man has no voice,
there shall be my voice.

Where blacks are flogged and beaten,
I cannot be dead.
When my brothers go to prison
I shall go with them.

When victory,
not my victory,
but the great victory
comes,
even if I am dumb I must speak;
I shall see it coming even if I am blind.

No, forgive me.
If you no longer live,
if you, beloved, my love,
if you
have died,
all the leaves will fall on my breast,
it will rain on my soul night and day,
the snow will burn my heart,
I shall walk with frost and fire and death and snow,
my feet will want to walk to where you are sleeping,
but
I shall stay alive,
because above all things you wanted me
indomitable,
and, my love, because you know that I am not only a man
but all mankind.

PABLO NERUDA (1904-73)
translated from the Spanish by Brian Cole

Every Town a Home Town

Every town our home town,
every man a kinsman.

Good and evil do not come
from others.
Pain and relief of pain
come of themselves.
Dying is nothing new.
We do not rejoice
that life is sweet
nor in anger
call it bitter.

Our lives, however dear,
follow their own course,
   rafts drifting
   in the rapids of a great river
   sounding and dashing over the rocks
   after a downpour
   from skies slashed by lightnings –

we know this
from the vision
of men who see.

So
we are not amazed by the great,
nor do we scorn the little.

KANIYAN PUNKUNRAN (*period* 100 BCE to 250 CE)
translated from the Tamil by A.K. Ramanujan

Begin

Begin again to the summoning birds
to the sight of light at the window,
begin to the roar of morning traffic
all along Pembroke Road.
Every beginning is a promise
born in light and dying in dark
determination and exaltation of springtime
flowering the way to work.
Begin to the pageant of queuing girls
the arrogant loneliness of swans in the canal
bridges linking the past and future
old friends passing though with us still.
Begin to the loneliness that cannot end
since it perhaps is what makes us begin,
begin to wonder at unknown faces
at crying birds in the sudden rain
at branches stark in the willing sunlight
at seagulls foraging for bread
at couples sharing a sunny secret
alone together while making good.
Though we live in a world that dreams of ending
that always seems about to give in
something that will not acknowledge conclusion
insists that we forever begin.

BRENDAN KENNELLY (*b.* 1936)

ACKNOWLEDGEMENTS

The poems in this anthology are reprinted from the following books, all by permission of the publishers listed unless stated otherwise. Thanks are due to all the copyright holders cited below for their kind permission:

Virginia Hamilton Adair: *Ants on the Melon* (Knopf, 1999), by permission of Random House, Inc; **Abu al-Ala al-Ma'arri:** *Birds Through a Ceiling of Alabaster: Three Abbasid Poets,* trs. Abdullah al-Udhari & George Wightman (Penguin Books, 1975), © Abdullah al-Udhari & George Wightman 1975, by permission of Abdullah al-Udhari; **W.H. Auden:** *Collected Poems,* ed. Edward Mendelson (Faber & Faber, 1991).

Basho: *The Penguin Book of Zen Poetry,* ed. & trs. Lucien Stryk & Takahashi Ikemoto (Penguin Books, 1977); **Wendell Berry:** *The Selected Poems of Wendell Berry* (Counterpoint, Washington, DC, 1998); **Bhartrhari:** *An Old Tree Living by the River: Poems of Bhartrhari,* trs. John Cort (Writers Workshop, Calcutta, 1983), by permission of John Cort.

Raymond Carver: *All of Us: Collected Poems* (Harvill Press, 1996), by permission of International Creative Management, Inc., copyright © 1996 Tess Gallagher; **Charles Causley:** *Collected Poems 1951-2000* (Picador, 2000), by permission of David Higham Associates Ltd; **Billy Collins:** *Taking Off Emily Dickinson's Clothes: Selected Poems* (Picador, 2000), by permission of Macmillan Publishers Ltd; **David Constantine:** *The Pelt of Wasps* (Bloodaxe Books, 1998).

Devara Dasimayya: *Speaking of Siva,* ed. & trs. A.K. Ramanujan (Penguin Books, India & USA, 1973); **Emily Dickinson:** *The Poems of Emily Dickinson,* ed. Ralph W. Franklin (Harvard University Press, 1998); **Stephen Dobyns:** *Common Carnage* (Penguin Books, USA, 1996; Bloodaxe Books, 1997), by permission of David Higham Associates Ltd and Viking Penguin.

D.J. Enright: *Collected Poems 1987* (Oxford University Press, 1987), by permission of Carcanet Press Ltd.

Janet Frame: *The Pocket Mirror* (The Women's Press, 1992), by permission of Curtis Brown Ltd.

Pamela Gillilan: *All-Steel Traveller: New & Selected Poems* (Bloodaxe Books, 1994); **Joyce Grenfell:** poem from *Joyce: By Herself and Her Friends* (Futura, 1980) by permission of Sheil Land Associates Ltd © The Joyce Grenfell Memorial Trust 1980; **Edgar A. Guest:** *The Collected Verse of Edgar A. Guest* (NTC/Contemporary Publishing Group, Lincolnwood, Illinois, 1984); **Thom Gunn:** *Collected Poems* (Faber & Faber, 1993).

Gail Holst-Warhaft: 'In the End Is the Body', reprinted from *The Gospels in Own Image* (Harcourt Brace, 1995), ed. David Curzon, by permission of the author; **Langston Hughes:** *The Collected Poems of Langston Hughes* (Knopf, NY, 1994), by permission of David Higham Associates and Random House Inc.

David Ignatow: *New and Selected Poems* (Wesleyan University Press, 1993); **Issa:** *The Penguin Book of Zen Poetry,* ed. & trs. by Lucien Stryk & Takahashi Ikemoto (Penguin Books, 1977).

Patrick Kavanagh: *Selected Poems,* ed. Antoinette Quinn (Penguin, 1996), reprinted here by permission of the Trustees of the Estate of the late Katherine B. Kavanagh, and through the Jonathan Williams Literary Agency; **Brendan Kennelly:** 'I See You Dancing Father' from *A Time for Voices: Selected Poems*

1960-1990 (Bloodaxe Books, 1990); 'Begin' from *Begin* (Bloodaxe Books, 1999); 'The Good' from *Breathing Spaces: Early Poems* (Bloodaxe Books, 1992); **Jane Kenyon:** *Otherwise: New & Selected Poems* (Graywolf Press, St Paul, Minnesota, 1996); **Rudyard Kipling:** *The Collected Works of Rudyard Kipling*, by permission of A.P. Watt Ltd.
 Philip Larkin: *Collected Poems*, ed. Anthony Thwaite (Faber & Faber, 1990); **D.H. Lawrence:** *Complete Poems* (Penguin Books, 1977), by permission of Pollinger Ltd and the Estate of Frieda Lawrence Ravagli.
 Norman MacCaig: *Collected Poems* (Chatto & Windus, 1990), by permission of the Random House Group Ltd; **Louis MacNeice:** *Collected Poems*, ed. E.R. Dodds (Faber, 1979), by permission of David Higham Associates Ltd; **Meera:** *Songs of Meera: In the Dark of the Heart*, trs. Shama Futehally (HarperCollins, USA, 1994), © 1994 Shama Futehally; **Czeslaw Milosz:** *New Collected Poems 1931-2001* (Ecco Press, USA; Penguin Books, 2001); **Adrian Mitchell:** *Blue Coffee: Poems 1985-1996* (Bloodaxe Books, 1996), by permission of Peters, Fraser & Dunlop, with an educational health warning: Adrian Mitchell asks that none of his poems be used in connection with any examination whatsoever; **Edwin Muir:** *Collected Poems* (Faber & Faber, 1984).
 Pablo Neruda: 'Dead Woman' from *The Captain's Verses*, translated by Brian Cole (Anvil Press Poetry, 1994); 'Sonnet LXXXIX' from *100 Love Sonnets*, translated by Stephen Tapscott (University of Texas Press, 1986); **Alden Nowlan:** *Selected Poems*, ed. Patrick Lane & Lorna Crozier (House of Anansi Press, Toronto, 1996).
 Hugh O'Donnell: 'Light' by permission of the author; **Mary Oliver:** 'When Death Comes' from *New and Selected Poems* (Beacon Press, 1992); 'In Blackwater Woods' from *American Primitive* (Little Brown, 1983), reprinted in *New and Selected Poems* (Beacon Press, 1992), both by permission of the publishers and the author.
 Linda Pastan: *The Five Stages of Grief* (W.W. Norton, 1978), reprinted in *Carnival Evening: New and Selected Poems 1968-1998* (W.W. Norton & Company, 1998); **Ruth Pitter:** *Collected Poems* (Enitharmon Press, 1990); **Patricia Pogson:** *Holding* (Flambard Press, 2002); **Kaniyan Punkunran:** *Poems of Love and War: from the Eight Anthologies and the Ten Long Poems in Classical Tamil*, ed. & trs. A.K. Ramanujan (Oxford University Press India; Columbia University Press, USA, 1985).
 Anne Ridler: *Collected Poems* (Carcanet Press, 1997); **Rumi:** 'Unmarked Boxes', trs. Coleman Barks & John Mayne, *The Essential Rumi* (HarperCollins, USA, 1995; Penguin Books, 1999), © Coleman Barks, also by permission of the Reid Boates Literary Agency; 'Why cling', trs. Daniel Liebert, *Fragments, Ecstasies* (Source Books, 1981; Omega Publications, 2000), by permission of Daniel Liebert and Omega Publications; 'Everything you see', trs. Andrew Harvey, *The Mystic Vision: Daily Encounters with the Divine*, ed. Andrew Harvey & Anne Baring (Godsfield Press, Alresford, Hants, 1995).
 Shiki: *The Penguin Book of Zen Poetry*, ed. & trs. by Lucien Stryk & Takahashi Ikemoto (Penguin Books, 1977); **Ken Smith:** *Shed: Poems 1980-2001* (Bloodaxe Books, 2002), **Stevie Smith:** *Collected Poems*, ed. James MacGibbon (Penguin, 1985), by permission of the James MacGibbon Estate and New Directions Publishing Corporation; **Anne Stevenson:** *Collected Poems 1955-1995* (Bloodaxe Books, 2000).
 Dylan Thomas: *Collected Poems* (J.M. Dent, 1988), by permission of David Higham Associates and New Directions Publishing Corporation; **R.S. Thomas:**

'A Marriage' from *Mass for Hard Times* (Bloodaxe Books, 1992); 'Comparisons' from *Residues* (Bloodaxe Books, 2002). **Mona Van Duyn:** *To See, To Take* (Atheneum, NY, 1970), reprinted in *If It Be Not I: Collected Poems 1959-1982* (Knopf, 1993) and in *Selected Poems* (Knopf, 2002), by permission of Random House Inc.

Alice Walker: *Her Blue Body Everything We Know: Earthling Poems 1960-1990 Complete* (Women's Press, 1991), reprinted by permission of David Higham Associates Ltd; **C.K. Williams:** 'Le Petit Salvié', parts 3-7, 9-11, from *New Selected Poems* (Farrar, Straus & Giroux, USA; Bloodaxe Books, 1995); 'Oh' and 'Wept' ('Elegy for an Artist', section 2) from *The Singing* (Farrar, Straus & Giroux, USA; Bloodaxe Books, 2003); **William Carlos Williams:** *Collected Poems I: 1909-1939* (Carcanet Press, 1987, 2000) by permission of Carcanet Press Ltd and New Directions Publishing Corporation; **Jeanne Willis:** *Toffee Pockets* (Bodley Head, 1992), by permission of the Random House Group Ltd; **David Wright:** *Collected Poems* (Carcanet Press, 1988).

Every effort has been made to trace copyright holders of the poems published in this book. The editor and publisher apologise if any material has been included without permission or without the appropriate acknowledgement, and would be glad to be told of anyone who has not been consulted.

American spellings are retained in poems by American writers.

QUOTATIONS

The short quotations of poetry and prose at the head of each section are from the following sources:

Francis Bacon (1561-1626): *Of Death.* **Bassui** (Zen Buddhist): words of comfort to a dying person. **Samuel Butler** (1835-1902): *Notebooks.* **John Fletcher** (1579-1625): poem: 'Fletcher's Lament for His Friend'. **William Hazlitt** (1778-1830): *On the Fear of Death.* **Carl Gustav Jung** (1878-1961): quoted in *The Mystic Vision*, ed. Andrew Harvey & Anne Baring (Godsfield Press, 1995). **Lao-tse** (*c.* 570 BC): from *The Wisdom of Lao-tse*, ed & trs Lin Yutang (Michael Joseph, London & Random House, Inc., New York). **Maurice Maeterlinck** (1862-1949): *Death*, trs. Alexander Teixeira de Mattos (Methuen). **Blaise Pascal** (1623-62): *Pensées.* **Theodore Roethke** (1908-63): poem: 'She', from *Collected Poems* (Faber, 1968). **Jahan Ramazani** (*b.* 1960): *Poetry of Mourning: The Modern Elegy from Hardy to Heaney* (University of Chicago Press, 1994). **Mevlâna Jalâluddin Rumi** (1207-73): Various sources. **Percy Bysshe Shelley** (1792-1822): poem: 'Adonais' (on the death of John Keats). **Sir Philip Sidney** (1554-86): poem: 'Against the fear of death'. **Dylan Thomas** (1914-53): poem: 'And Death Shall Have No Dominion'. **Walt Whitman** (1819-92): poem: 'When lilacs last in the dooryard bloom'd'.

SPECIAL THANKS

I would like to thank Imogen Stubbs for suggesting this book; and for their many helpful suggestions of poems for inclusion: Lord Carey of Clifton, David Constantine, Imtiaz Dharker, Simon & Gwennie Fraser, Brendan Kennelly and David Scott; and for their anthologies and critical studies: Elspeth Barker, Rachel R. Baum, June Benn, Judi Benson & Agneta Falk, Carol Ann Duffy, Jahan Ramazani, Peter Washington and Agnes Whitaker.

INDEX OF WRITERS

Staying Alive
real poems for unreal times
edited by NEIL ASTLEY

Staying Alive is an international anthology of 500 life-affirming poems fired by belief in the human and the spiritual at a time when much in the world feels unreal, inhuman and hollow. These are poems of great personal force connecting our aspirations with our humanity, helping us stay alive to the world and stay true to ourselves.

'*Staying Alive* is a blessing of a book. The title says it all. I have long waited for just this kind of setting down of poems. Has there ever been such a passionate anthology? These are poems that hunt you down with the solace of their recognition' – ANNE MICHAELS.

'*Staying Alive* is a book which leaves those who have read or heard a poem from it feeling less alone and more alive' – JOHN BERGER.

'*Staying Alive* is a magnificent anthology. The last time I was so excited, engaged and enthralled by a collection of poems was when I first encountered *The Rattle Bag*' – PHILIP PULLMAN

'A vibrant, brilliantly diverse anthology of poems to delight the mind, heart and soul. A book for people who know they love poetry, and for people who think they don't' – HELEN DUNMORE.

'Usually if you say a book is "inspirational" that means it's New Agey and soft at the center. This astonishingly rich anthology, by contrast, shows that what is edgy, authentic and provocative can also awaken the spirit and make its readers quick with consciousness' – EDMUND WHITE.

'This is a book to make you fall in love with poetry...Go out and buy it for everyone you love' – CHRISTINA PATTERSON, *Independent*.

'Anyone who has the faintest glimmer of interest in modern poetry must buy it. If I were master of the universe or held the lottery's purse strings, there would be a copy of it in every school, public library and hotel bedroom in the land...I found myself laughing, crying, wondering, rejoicing, reliving, wishing, envying. It is a book full of hope and high art which restores your faith in poetry' – ALAN TAYLOR, *Sunday Herald*.

'These poems, just words, distil the human heart as nothing else' – JANE CAMPION.